How Do We Use Scientific Investigation and Reasoning?

HOUGHTON MIFFLIN HARCOURT

ISBN: 978-0-544-07312-8

6 7 8 9 10 0908 21 20 19 18 17 16

4500608014   A B C D E F G

Be an Active Reader!

 Look at these words.

scientist	evidence	two-dimensional model
observation	inference	three-dimensional model
investigation	empirical evidence	computer model
data	microscope	
hypothesis	model	

Look for answers to these questions.

What is a scientist?

Why do scientists ask questions?

How do scientists answer questions?

How do scientists answer questions when they can't use an investigation?

Why do scientists communicate their results?

What inquiry skills do scientists use?

What are critical thinking skills?

How do scientists collect data?

How do scientists organize data?

How do scientists analyze data?

Which tools do scientists use to collect data?

How do scientists measure?

How do scientists use models?

What is a scientist?

A scientist is a person who asks questions about the natural world and how it works. Science is the study of the natural world. There are different kinds of science. Life science is the study of living things. Physical science is the study of matter. Earth science is the study of the Earth's surface, its interior, the oceans, and the atmosphere.

Scientists have always asked questions. Many of the questions scientists of long ago asked have been answered. Do the planets orbit the Earth? No. Does Earth orbit the sun? Yes. Scientists build on what people before them have discovered and learned. But there are still countless questions that scientists today can ask and try to answer.

You're acting like a scientist when you ask questions about organisms you observe in a terrarium or aquarium.

Why do scientists ask questions?

Scientists start with questions when they want to learn something about the natural world. The questions they ask will help them investigate, or look for answers. You can ask questions, too. You might ask, "Why does a cat purr?" or "Do birds have a sense of smell?" You probably have many questions about how the natural world works.

Scientists start to answer their questions by making observations. An observation is information collected through the five senses: sight, hearing, smell, taste, and touch. Scientists improve and focus their questions based on the observations they make. What they observe with their senses gives them important information.

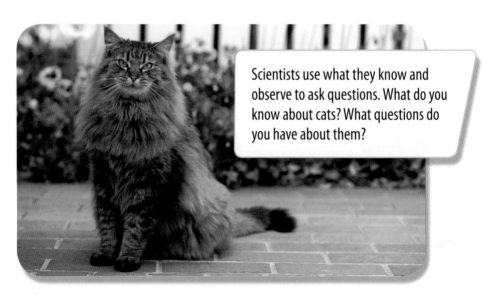

Scientists use what they know and observe to ask questions. What do you know about cats? What questions do you have about them?

Students are testing their hypothesis that an indoor plant will grow faster under a grow light than in indirect sunlight.

How do scientists answer questions?

Scientists carry out an investigation to answer questions. Investigations are procedures, or actions, carried out to gather data, or information.

Students in science class wonder, "Will plants grow faster under a grow light or near sunlight?" They begin with a hypothesis, an idea that can be tested with an investigation. The students state their hypothesis: "Plants will grow faster under a grow light than in indirect sunlight." The class takes measurements every day. The data they collect will be evidence that shows whether or not their hypothesis was supported.

Scientists used data and pictures to help answer this question, "What are Saturn's rings made of?"

How do scientists answer questions when they can't use an investigation?

Scientists cannot answer every question with an investigation. For example, they might ask, "What type of fish is this?" This question is answered with research. Research involves reading what others have written and talking to experts.

You might want to know "What causes day and night?" This cannot be answered with an experiment. To answer this question you need to build a model.

Another question you might want to ask is, "What time of year is the windiest?" You would answer this question by looking at weather records.

Why do scientists communicate their results?

Scientists share their results. A scientist who finds a cure for a disease would write about it. The discovery might be published in a science journal. The scientist would tell other scientists at work and at conferences. Other scientists could repeat the experiment. They could compare results.

When scientists share their results, they include data. Data is information gathered in an investigation. For example, think about the students and their experiment with the grow light. The students' data showed that plants grew faster under grow lights than in indirect sunlight.

One way scientists communicate their results is by presenting information at conferences.

What inquiry skills do scientists use?

Scientists use inquiry skills. The main inquiry skills are observing, inferring, comparing, deciding, and communicating. You use observing skills when you use your senses to get information. You observe that your dog is wet after a trip outside. From this observation, you might infer that it is raining. An inference is a statement that explains an observation or a result.

Scientists also compare objects and events. When you compare objects, you tell how they are the same and different. Compare the two animals below. Which one would make a better pet for a small apartment? Communicate your reasons by speaking or writing about them.

Which animal would make a better pet for a small apartment? Why?

Scientists ask a question and develop a hypothesis. Then they plan and carry out an experiment, a test done under controlled conditions, to see if the hypothesis is supported by data. Suppose you want to know: "Does water or juice freeze faster?" First, you use what you know to predict what will happen. Then, you think of a hypothesis: "Juice will freeze faster than water." Next, you plan the experiment. In an experiment, only one factor, or variable, can change. The variable is the kind of liquid that is used. You put exactly one cup of each liquid in the freezer. You check the freezer every 10 minutes. The water froze first. You repeat the experiment to see if you get similar results. If your data didn't support your hypothesis, that's okay. You state the results: Water freezes faster than juice.

A student wants to test her hypothesis that juice will freeze faster than water.

What are critical thinking skills?

Have you ever compared two books, or made a decision about which athletic shoes were best for gym class? Have you ever invented a new game or thought of a way to make more storage space in your room? When you do these things, you're using critical thinking skills. Critical thinking means that you think about facts and draw your own conclusions.

Scientists also use critical thinking skills to evaluate data. They use these skills to decide if a conclusion is reasonable. In an investigation, conclusions are based on empirical evidence. Empirical evidence is data collected through direct observation. Scientists use empirical evidence when they review, analyze, and evaluate investigations.

Measuring is a method of collecting empirical evidence.

One way that scientists study volcanoes is through observational testing.

Logical Reasoning Logical reasoning allows you to draw conclusions based on facts. For example, on your way to school you see dark clouds in the sky. Later, in class, you hear a loud boom in the distance. You use what you observed and what you know to draw the conclusion that the boom is thunder.

Experimental Testing Suppose you want to find out how much water a plant needs to grow. You design an experiment to answer the question. You collect data and analyze it to answer the question.

Observational Testing Scientists can't answer a question such as "How are rocks formed?" with an experiment. To answer such questions, scientists have to observe and measure nature over time.

Scientists use tools to collect data. They make observations and take measurements.

How do scientists collect data?

An important part of science is collecting data. Scientists collect data when they draw a plant. They collect data when they count how many tadpoles hatch from a frog's eggs.

Scientists use tools to collect data. They use hand lenses to observe objects up close and metric rulers to measure height, length, and width. They use spring scales to measure force and Celsius thermometers to measure temperature.

In daily life, we often speak in terms of pounds, feet, and ounces. Scientists use the metric system to measure weight, length, and volume. Grams, meters, and liters are all metric units of measure.

How do scientists organize data?

Scientists use tables, charts, graphs, and maps to organize data. They also use computer software.

Graphs make it easy to notice patterns. Different types of graphs include bar, line graphs, and picture graphs.

You can also use maps. Geographic maps show land and sea. Weather maps show weather in different places. To organize data, use a concept map.

Tables organize numerical data.

Average High Temperature in Texas	
Month	**Temperature**
August	36°C
September	32°C
October	27°C
November	21°C
December	17°C

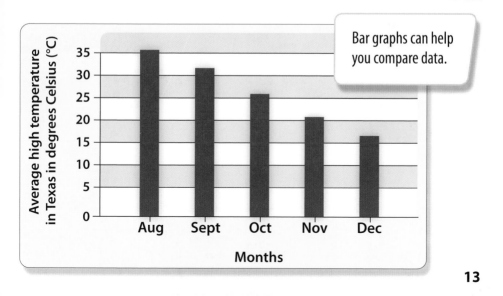

Bar graphs can help you compare data.

How do scientists analyze data?

Scientists must figure out what their data means. Math skills are important when the data involves numbers. Scientists look for patterns in data. They might identify a trend or a direction. For example, after looking at weather data for months, scientists might see that less rain is falling. They might try to explain why.

Scientists also check their data for errors. They compare their data to data from other sources. They also review the procedures they used. They make sure that they completed each step correctly. If they find errors, they must repeat the experiment.

Scientists use computers to analyze data.

Computers and other technology can help you record and analyze data as scientists do.

Next, scientists draw conclusions. Remember that a conclusion must be supported by data. The more data scientists have, the stronger the conclusion.

Next, scientists must decide if the hypothesis is supported by the data or not. If the hypothesis is supported, the experiment will need to be repeated. Scientists want to see if they get similar results. If the hypothesis is not supported, scientists will try and rethink their hypothesis. They will often form a new hypothesis. Then they will do a new experiment.

Which tools do scientists use to collect data?

Scientists use tools to make their observations easier. Tools can be as simple as a notebook or as complex as a computer. Both can be used to record and analyze data.

A hand lens is one type of tool scientists use to look closely at objects. If scientists want to get an even closer look, they use a microscope. A microscope is a tool for looking at objects that cannot be seen with the eyes alone. It is much more powerful than a hand lens.

A hand lens allows you to closely observe an object.

You can observe creatures and release them unharmed when you use a collecting net.

Suppose scientists want to get a closer look at a fish. They might use a collecting net. They pull the net through the water to catch the fish. Then they can observe the fish and later return it to the water.

Another tool that helps scientists make observations is a camera. A camera helps scientists observe and record changes that happen. Sometimes it is hard to see things that change very slowly or very quickly. Photos and video can help keep track of these changes.

Scientists may record their observations in notebooks. They might include drawings with their written notes. They may also use computers or tablets to record their observations.

How do scientists measure?

There are different tools to measure different objects. Measuring makes data more exact. Scientists use the metric system of measurement. A metric ruler measures length or distance. There are also tools to measure mass, force, volume, temperature, and time. A pan balance measures mass with units called grams (g). A triple beam balance can also measure mass. A spring scale measures force in units called newtons (N). Celsius thermometers measure temperature. Clocks and stopwatches are tools that measure time.

Use a metric ruler to measure the height or length of objects.

Scientists use many different tools in the lab.

Scientists use a variety of tools in laboratories. For example, scientists might need to measure and mix two different liquids. They use graduated cylinders to measure the volume of liquids. They use beakers to mix liquids together. They might also use a hot plate to warm the liquids.

Sometimes scientists conduct experiments on objects that cannot be touched. You might want to learn about light, but you can't touch it. A mirror can help you see how light reflects. A lens can help you understand how light bends. You might want to test the properties of an object. You could use a magnet to find out which materials are magnetic.

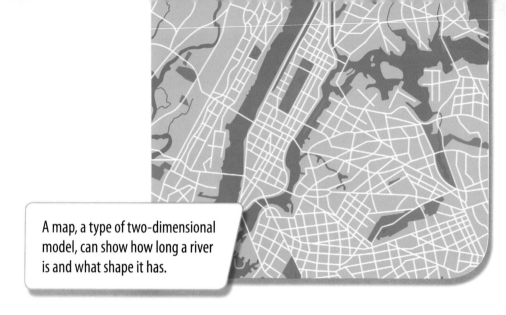

A map, a type of two-dimensional model, can show how long a river is and what shape it has.

How do scientists use models?

Sometimes experiments cannot be done on real objects. In science, a model represents an object that is too big, too small, or has too many parts to test directly. Scientists draw conclusions and make predictions about these objects by using models.

For example, a river can be hundreds of miles long. Its size makes it hard to study. Something that takes several days to see in a river could take just a few minutes in a model.

There are different types of models. Drawings, diagrams, and maps can be models. Each is a two-dimensional model because it shows only length and width.

The more a model is like the real object, the more useful it is. Sometimes scientists will use a three-dimensional model, which has length, width, and height. A stream table, for example, is a three-dimensional model that scientists can use to observe the properties of moving water.

Suppose you wanted to understand how the river flows during different types of weather. A stream table could not show this. Instead, you could use a computer model. A computer model is a computer program that models an event or a process. It can show how events or conditions might change over time.

Even good models have limitations. A three-dimensional model of a dinosaur could show what the animal looked like. But it could not show how the animal behaved. It could not tell us what sounds the animal made or what it smelled like.

A stream table is a type of three-dimensional model. A stream table can model properties of flowing water. A map could not show this.

Plan and Conduct an Investigation

Plan and carry out an investigation to answer a question. Write down a question you would like to investigate. For example, you might want to investigate what kinds of birds visit a bird feeder in a particular season. Write down the plan that you will follow to answer the question. Be sure to get your teacher's permission to carry out the plan. Make a list of any materials that you will need. Collect and record your data in a chart or table. Analyze the data and draw a conclusion. Communicate your results.

Write About a Scientist

Use the Internet to find out about a scientist. The scientist can be living or historical. Find out what kind of scientist this person is and what contributions he or she has made to science. Record several interesting facts about this scientist. Draw a picture to show his or her achievements in science. Share your facts with your classmates.

Glossary

computer model [kuhm•PYOO•ter MAH•duhl] A computer program that models an event or object.

data [DAY•tuh] Individual facts, statistics, and items of information.

empirical evidence [im•PIR•uh•kuhl EV•uh•duhns] Data collected through direct observation.

evidence [EV•uh•duhns] Data gathered in an investigation.

hypothesis [hy•POTH•i•sis] A possible explanation or answer to a question; a testable statement.

inference [IN•fer•uhns] An untested conclusion based on your observations.

investigation [in•ves•tuh•GAY•shuhn] A procedure carried out to gather data about an object or event.

microscope [MY•kruh•skohp] A tool that makes an object look several times bigger than it is.

model [MAHD•L] A representation of something real that is too big, too small, or has too many parts to investigate directly.

observation [ahb•zer•VAY•shuhn] Information collected by using one or more of the five senses.

scientist [SY•uhn•tist] A person who asks questions about the natural world.

three-dimensional model [THREE di•MEN•shuh•nuhl MAHD•L] A model that has the dimension of height as well as width and length.

two-dimensional model [TOO di•MEN•shuh•nuhl MAHD•L] A model that has the dimensions of length and width.